Fun with
Calligraphy

*Reviewed and endorsed by Nancy McCarthy, calligraphy instructor, Arts
Unlimited, Chadwick School, Palos Verdes Peninsula, California*

By Sharon McCoy and Sheryl Scarborough

Calligraphy and illustrations by Wesla Weller

Lowell House
Juvenile
Los Angeles

CONTEMPORARY BOOKS
Chicago

ISBN: 1-56565-203-7

Library of Congress Catalog Card Number: 94-31890

Publisher: Jack Artenstein
General Manager, Juvenile Division: Elizabeth D. Wood
Editorial Director: Brenda Pope-Ostrow
Director of Publishing Services: Mary D. Aarons
Senior Editor: Amy Downing
Art Director: Lisa-Theresa Lenthall
Text Design: Brenda Leach
Cover Photograph: Chuck Potter

Manufactured in the United States of America

10 9 8 7 6 5 4 3 2

Contents

What Is Calligraphy?

The art of calligraphy is as old as the pyramids in Egypt, which is where decorative writing first began. In ancient Egypt, stories were put in writing using a series of pictures called hieroglyphs. These pictures eventually evolved into symbols or letters that look a lot like today's alphabet.

In the time of ancient Egypt, most people did not know how to write at all, much less how to write beautifully. People who could write calligraphy, who were known as calligraphers, were considered very important because they were able to record the exploits of kings for future generations to read.

As printing technology has progressed over the years, many calligraphers have feared that the fine art of handwriting might be lost. Fortunately, this hasn't happened. Even with the number of high-tech tools available for lettering today, especially computers, people young and old still learn and use calligraphy for the sheer enjoyment and beauty of the art.

Calligraphy can be profitable, too. Kids can earn money in their spare time by designing documents for others, just as ancient calligraphers received money and gifts by writing for kings!

As you learn basic calligraphy styles, you'll discover all kinds of creative ways to put your new skill to use. To get you started, this book will teach you how to make table place cards, fold-it notecards, invitations, a personalized happy birthday poster card, and more.

Are you ready to grab your calligraphy pen and begin? Write on!

CHAPTER 1

Calligraphy Tools and Techniques

C alligraphy is not difficult to master, but it does require practice, the right tools, and the ability to follow instructions. This chapter will introduce the basic tools you'll need as well as exercises to get you started.

Getting Started

Calligraphy looks different from the writing you do every day, because each calligraphy stroke has both wide and narrow parts to it. This effect is achieved by using a special pen with a broad, flat tip.

Several types of pens work well for calligraphy. For this book, you will want to use a dual-tipped marker with a broad, flat tip on one end and a brush on the other, designed especially for calligraphers. You can find pens like this one in a variety of colors at most art-supply stores.

Two other kinds of calligraphy tools, fountain pens and calligraphy pens, can also be used. They will cost more but will last longer because they have a metal tip. A fountain pen can be refilled over and over with ink, whereas a calligraphy pen works something like a paintbrush: you dip the tip of the pen into a bottle of ink and move it to the paper to make your stroke.

fountain pen   calligraphy pen   flat-tipped calligraphy marker

Proper Posture

Correct posture, or how you sit, while doing calligraphy may not seem important, but it is actually the first step to creating beautiful artwork.

You need to sit in a comfortable chair at a table or desk where there is good light. To avoid creating a shadow on your work, position the light to come from your left side. (If you are left-handed, position the light to your right.) Sit up straight, then turn your body to the left about one-third of the way around (turn to the right if you are left-handed). Be sure your body is relaxed. If you feel tense, it will show in your work.

Setting Up Your Work Space

Place a stack of about ten sheets of lined notebook paper in front of you, and tilt the top of them toward your left side so they are lined up with the way you are sitting. (If you are left-handed, see page 9 for tips on the best position for you.)

Grip the pen in your hand as you would hold a pencil: between your thumb and index finger, with the lower part of the pen  resting on your middle finger for support. You should hold the pen so lightly that someone could lift it out of your hand.

To learn the difference between how you write every day and how a calligrapher writes, use your normal cursive or block handwriting to fill in the lines below with your name, your age, and your favorite color. While you are writing, notice how your wrist and fingers do most of the work as the pen moves across the paper.

My name: _____

My age: _____

My favorite color: _____

When you begin writing calligraphy, you will use a completely different motion. Your shoulder will control the movement of your arm and hand as you write. To practice this motion, pretend that the pen and your hand, fingers, wrist, and forearm are a solid block of wood. Your elbow will move the "block of wood" from side to side, while your shoulder will move it up and down. Move your arm and pen around as one unit without putting your pen on the paper. Now try writing your best friend's name on the line below to test out your new grip, posture, and movement.

My best friend's name: _____

   In calligraphy, you don't move your hand down to the next line. Instead, you move the paper up so that your hand and arm remain in roughly the same writing position.

   Once you get used to this writing position, you may be surprised to find that it is less tiring than the one you use with your usual writing style.

What if You Are Left-Handed?

If you are left-handed, the above instructions for posture, pen grip, and angle of paper might not give you the best results. The challenge for left-handers is to get the right posture and angle for the pen to stroke the paper. There are many lefties who excel at calligraphy by using special tricks. Here are a couple of different suggestions for positioning the paper if you are left-handed:

1. With your calligraphy marker in your left hand, turn the top of the paper all the way to the right. Hold the paper in place with your right hand as shown.

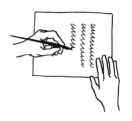

2. Position the paper with the top tilted to the left and hold it in place with your right hand. Place the pen in your left hand, then hook your arm and hand over the top of the paper and form the letters from left to right.

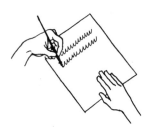

There is no one perfect position for left-handers. Feel free to experiment to find the position that works best for you.

Lining Up

When you write on regular notebook paper, you use the lines on the paper to keep your words from sloping up or down. In calligraphy, you also use lines, not only to keep your words straight but also to help you make sure the words are the right height. The four different lines you need to know are listed below.

ascender line
waist line
base line
descender line

hyo

"C" Stands for Control

You're probably anxious to start lettering, but first you need to just get the feel of the pen and the strokes. At first you won't be creating actual letters, but each exercise, called Writing Workout, builds upon the other.

Don't skip over any of the following exercises. For each assignment in this book, you should follow these steps:

1. *Study* each new exercise.

2. *Trace* the strokes and letters to understand how they are formed.

3. *Draw* the strokes on your own so you can see how well you are progressing.

Before you get started with any Writing Workout, make sure you have all the necessary tools: several sheets of 8½-by-11-inch tracing paper, paper clips, and your calligraphy marker. Have lined notebook paper handy as well for extra practice.

WRITING WORKOUT:

The following exercises will help you get used to writing with your calligraphy marker. The arrows in each exercise will show you the direction in which to draw your lines, and the numbers will show which line to draw first, second, and so on.

It is important to keep the wedge tip of the pen in the same position and angle throughout the stroke. This is what makes the lines of the stroke both thin and wide. Also, keep the direction of the stroke consistent, and make sure each stroke touches both the upper and lower guidelines.

DOWNSTROKES: This exercise will teach you how to make a slightly slanted *downward* stroke. First, trace the downstrokes, keeping the slant even. Your pen should move smoothly on the paper. If it sticks, skips, or jerks, you are probably gripping the pen too tightly or your hand is too tense. Remember to relax.

After you have traced the downstrokes once, try drawing a line of them free-hand on the lines below. Keep practicing until you feel comfortable before you move on.

DIAGONAL STROKES: In this exercise, you will first do the downward stroke you learned above, then add a diagonal *upward* stroke, followed by another *downward* stroke. Trace first, then practice these strokes (which look like backward Ns) on the lines below until you feel comfortable. Remember, every stroke must touch the top and bottom guidelines.

MAKING THE CONNECTION: Now you'll combine the strokes you learned on the previous page into one long, fluid design. While tracing, move along at an even pace. You should begin to develop a sense of how to keep the strokes the same distance apart. This will be important later, when you are learning to control the look of your work. When you are ready, practice the connecting strokes on the lines below.

DOUBLE DIAGONAL STROKES: These are both upward and downward diagonal strokes that are created with one fluid motion. Study the numbered arrows and follow their direction. Trace the strokes first, then draw them on the lines below.

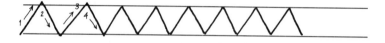

Ready for a self-test? You can check how well you are spacing between strokes by filling in the triangle-shaped peaks above. Fill in the triangles on your practice lines. These colored-in blocks should look as even as possible.

The next group of exercises will blend together downstrokes and curves.

DOWNSTROKE WITH HUMP: In this exercise, you will connect a curved stroke to the downward stroke. Trace first the straight downward line, then lift your pen to add the second, curved stroke. Once you are comfortable, practice these exercises on the lines below. Remember, don't hold the pen too tightly. Relax!

n n n n n n n n n

DOWNSTROKE WITH REVERSED HUMP: Now you will reverse the hump you drew above, making it u-shaped. Follow the arrows for direction and concentrate on keeping each shape the same size. As before, trace the lines first, then draw them on the lines below. Compare your work with the illustration to see how you are improving. Don't forget to use your shoulder to control the movement of your arm and hand as you write.

u u u u u u u u u

Border Design

Have some fun and master your strokes at the same time by combining practice strokes into an interesting border for an already existing picture frame.

MATERIALS:

- ruler
- pencil
- 8-by-10-inch sheet of white paper
- black calligraphy marker
- colored markers or pencils

DIRECTIONS:

1. Use the pencil and ruler to lightly draw a box measuring exactly 1 inch in from the edge of the paper. This 1-inch area will become your border.

2. Pick a border design from the samples below or make up one of your own to go around the border of your paper. Now, with your black calligraphy marker, start at the top left-hand corner and make your design all the way across the top of the page, using the pencil line as your base line. Stop when you come to the right-hand corner.

3. Allow the ink to dry for at least 30 minutes. Then turn the paper so that the side you just inked is on your right. Once again, start at the left, making the practice strokes along the pencil line. When you come to the corner, stop.

4. Repeat steps 2 and 3 until you are finished making each side of the border.

5. Wait for the ink to dry, then gently erase the light pencil lines. Now, decorate your border design using colorful markers or pencils. When you are finished, you will have an unusual, one-of-a-kind border design that will fit inside your favorite 8-by-10-inch picture frame.

Take this tip:

Within the border, you can center a photograph and attach it with a little bit of glue. Or you can cut carefully along the inside edge of your border and place the border over your photograph before inserting both into the picture frame.

CHAPTER 2

Basic Chancery Italics

Get set to impress your friends and family by mastering the basics of calligraphy! The Basic Chancery Italic style was developed in Italy and is fun to do because it's so graceful and uncomplicated. You'll learn to recognize its distinct form by the way it slants to the right and by its absence of heavy flourishes. (Flourishes are the decorative hooks that begin and/or end each letter.)

Because this calligraphy style is so easy to read, you can use it for everyday types of correspondence. Try using Basic Chancery Italics to print name tags, cards, letters, informal invitations, and even homework assignments.

Lowercase Letters

There are three basic kinds of lowercase letters, called minuscules, used in the Basic Chancery Italic style: ascenders (letters that extend above the waist line), descenders (letters that extend below the base line), and centered minuscules (letters that sit squarely between the waist line and base line).

a b c d e f g h i j k l m n

o p q r s t u v w x y z

Between the Lines

First we'll focus on the centered minuscules: *a, c, e, i, m, n, o, r, s, u, v, w, x,* and *z.* Note that the letters *i, m, n, u, x,* and *z* receive a soft hook at the beginning of the first stroke and also a soft, small flourish or hook at the end. The letters *r, v,* and *w* receive a soft hook only at the beginning of the first stroke.

WRITING WORKOUT:

Ready to practice tracing? Paper-clip a sheet of tracing paper over the letters illustrated below and draw each letter, following the arrows. Strive for a consistent pace and use only moderate pressure. Remember, you're new at this, so don't expect perfection overnight! (If you're feeling unsure of the position of your hand or your posture, review page 8 in chapter 1.)

a c e i m n o r

s u v w x z

After tracing each character, stop and review your work. Are you comfortable tracing the letters, even though they may not look perfect? If so, try drawing each of these letters in between the base and waist lines below, referring to the illustration above for direction. To make your spacing uniform between the letters, imagine a space the size of one letter *o* between each character. No matter how perfectly a letter is formed, beautiful calligraphy is not possible unless it is spaced properly.

Above and Below the Line

Let's take a closer look at the remaining lowercase letters. Ascenders are those letters that extend above the waist line to reach the ascender line: *b, d, f* (also a descender), *h, k,* and *l*. The letter *t* is also considered an ascender even though it doesn't reach the ascender line. Descenders are those letters that extend below the base line to reach the descender line: *f, g, j, p, q,* and *y*.

*W*RITING WORKOUT:

Paper-clip a sheet of tracing paper over the letters below. Practice writing each ascender and descender by tracing it in the direction of the arrows. Try to trace at a consistent pace, using only moderate pressure.

Review the letters you've just traced. Are the lines smooth and even? Keep tracing until your letters look similar to the ones drawn above. Then, using the lines below, draw each letter on your own.

Capitals Count!

In the Basic Chancery Italic hand, capital letters have longer hooks than the lowercase alphabet. They also extend from the base line to the halfway point between the ascender line and the waist line. Notice that there is only one ascender in the uppercase alphabet: *H* (which should extend to the ascender line), and only four descenders: *G, J, Q,* and *Y* (which fall just above the descender line). All other capital letters sit squarely between the top dotted line and the base line.

*W*RITING WORKOUT:

Since the uppercase letters have longer hooks and more elaborate strokes, pay close attention to the direction of the arrows. Paper-clip a sheet of tracing paper over the letters below and use only moderate pressure to trace the alphabet. Be sure to lift your pen off the paper each time you change direction.

How comfortable do you feel tracing the uppercase letters? If you still feel a little unsure, go back and trace the uppercase alphabet again until the strokes feel natural. Then, on the lines below, try making the letters on your own. (Remember, all of the letters except for *H* extend only halfway between the waist line and the ascender line). If you run out of room here or if you want more practice, use lined notebook paper.

Joining Letters

Now that you know how to draw all the letters of the alphabet, you're ready to begin connecting them. This brings you one step closer to creating beautiful calligraphy artwork.

In the Basic Chancery Italic hand, you will join the lowercase letters that end with the last stroke swinging in a soft hook on the base line: *a, c, d, e, h, i, k, l, m, n,* and *u*. Each time you use one of these letters, you'll join it to the next letter in the word by carrying the soft hook up to meet the next letter, as shown below. In Basic Chancery Italics, only these eleven letters join with whatever letter follows. The remaining fifteen letters stand alone, because they do not have hooks on the end to connect them to another letter on the right. For instance, in the word *basic,* the *a* will connect to the *s,* and the *i* will connect to the *c.*

WRITING WORKOUT:

Printed below are the eleven lowercase letters that have soft hooks and therefore can be connected in the Basic Chancery Italic alphabet. Paper-clip a sheet of tracing paper over the letters and trace each one, joining them on the base line as shown.

acdehiklmnu

Are you ready to join letters on your own? For practice, print out the entire lowercase alphabet below and connect only those letters that should be joined. (The *a* joins with the *b*, the *b* does not join to the *c*, the *c* connects to the *d*, and so on.)

Putting It All Together

It's time to put together all the information you've learned in this chapter to create a sentence! This is a challenging calligraphy exercise, so take your time, and remember, patience counts!

*W*RITING WORKOUT:

Paper-clip a sheet of tracing paper over the sentence below. Trace all the printed words, joining letters where necessary. (You may need to remind yourself as to the order of the strokes or the direction in which the strokes are made. Turn to pages 17 and 20 for help.) After you've traced the sentence, write it on your own on the lines provided on the next page. It may take several tries to get a polished product, so if at first you don't get the results you want, keep trying!

What counts in calligraphy is not the number of hours you put in, but how much you put in the hours.

The Perfect Mealtime Place Cards

Add some flair to the table settings at your next family holiday meal by making these calligraphy place cards for each member of the clan!

MATERIALS:
- lined notebook paper for practicing
- one unlined 3-by-5-inch index card for each person
- ruler
- pencil
- black calligraphy marker
- soft eraser

DIRECTIONS:

1. To begin, fold each index card in half lengthwise to create place cards, then unfold the cards to write on them.

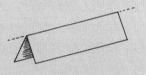

2. Use a ruler to measure and a pencil to draw the lines shown below on the bottom half of each card. You'll use these lines as a guide when you write each name on the place cards.

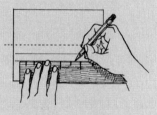

_____

_____

----

3. Now practice writing each person's first name on the scratch paper using the Basic Chancery Italic alphabet. Be certain that you make the first capital letter of the name larger than the remaining lowercase letters. Except for the letter *H*, every capital letter should

reach halfway between the waist line and the ascender line. If necessary, first trace the letters for more practice.

4. Once you feel comfortable creating the names, write them with your calligraphy marker on the place cards, using the pencil lines as a guide. Allow the ink to dry on each place card for about 30 minutes, then carefully erase the pencil lines.

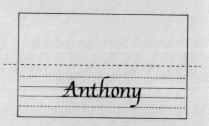

5. Refold each card in half to create place cards for the table. When you set out the cards for your next big family dinner, your calligraphy will be displayed for all to see!

The Numbers Game

Now that you are familiar with the Basic Chancery Italic letters, it's time to learn the Chancery numbers. Once you know how to make numbers, you can print addresses, birthdays, and dates with ease. Just think about all the invitations, cards, and other cool gifts you can create on your own. Notice that the numbers *3, 6,* and *8* rise slightly above the waist line, while *4, 5,* and *9* extend below the base line. All the other numbers sit squarely between the waist line and the base line.

*W*RITING WORKOUT:

Paper-clip a sheet of tracing paper over the numbers below. Trace the numbers following the direction of the arrows.

1 2 3 4 5 6 7 8 9 0

How do your figures look? Are you ready to strike out on your own and draw them freehand? On the lines below, create the numbers *0* through *9*.

Happening Holiday Cards

Why blow a bundle at the stationery shop buying pre-made holiday cards when you can create your own in a snap? Send these creative cards and give friends and family alike a glimpse of your true talent!

MATERIALS:
- one 8½-by-11-inch piece of white construction paper for each card
- scratch paper
- black calligraphy brush marker
- pencil
- newspaper
- clear-drying glue in a tube

- two shades of glitter in coordinating colors (blue and gold, red and silver, etc.)

DIRECTIONS:

1. First, create blank cards by folding each sheet of white construction paper in half from top to bottom as shown. Set these aside. Then, decide on a message for your card. Here are a few ideas: "Here's to a Wild and Wacky New Year!"; "Season's Greetings to My Best Bud!"; "May the Spirit of the Season Make You Smile." Once you've chosen a phrase, practice writing it on the scratch paper using your brush marker. (Hold your brush pen in the same way you hold your calligraphy marker.)

2. When you're happy with the message, lightly pencil in guidelines onto the front of your construction paper. The four guidelines can be spaced as far apart as you choose, but each line should be equally spaced. (The bigger the width, the larger your letters will be.)

3. In your best calligraphy, write your message on the cards. Once the ink dries, open each card and write a personal message in calligraphy. It can be as simple as: "Love, (your name)." Do this on all the holiday cards.

4. Allow the ink inside the cards to dry. Meanwhile, lay the newspaper on a flat work surface.

5. When the ink has dried, decorate your card by squirting glue directly onto the card in any pattern you like, then liberally sprinkle glitter over the glue. You can make a border around the phrase on the front, draw the outline of something related to the holidays (such as a bell, angel, holly, or reindeer) or even create abstract lines and squiggles.

6. Once you've covered the glue with glitter, let it sit for a few minutes, then pick up the card and shake off any excess glitter onto the newspaper. Don't forget to use both shades of glitter! You can even open up the card and use glitter to decorate the page where you signed your name. These beautiful handmade cards are sure to add sparkle to everyone's holiday season!

CHAPTER 3

Basic Formal Script

*B*asic Formal Script, characterized by straight up-and-down strokes, is a widely used calligraphy style. The letters have an elegant simplicity, and once you learn the basics, you can use the alphabet any way you like to create sensational pieces of art.

A unique aspect of this style is that it does not contain any capital letters, which gives the alphabet an artistic, classic look. You'll find that the letters in the Basic Formal Script are wider and heavier than those in the Basic Chancery Italic style that you learned in the previous chapter.

The Lowercase Alphabet

Except for the small serifs on ascenders and descenders, there are no heavy flourishes to learn in Basic Formal Script. A serif, like a flourish, is the beginning or ending stroke of a letter, but it is much simpler than the more elaborate flourish. Notice on the following page that the strokes of the letters below are vertical, not slanted; short, not tall; and round, not narrow.

Check how the body of each letter fills a $\frac{1}{4}$-inch square, with the exception of *m* and *w*, which fill two squares. The ascenders *b, d, f, h, k, l,* and *t* extend above the square, and the descenders *f, g, j, p, q,* and *y* extend below the square. The ascenders and descenders must be drawn shorter than those in the previous chapter in order to achieve the short, round look of the Basic Formal Script hand.

a b c d e f g h i
j k k l m n o p q
r s t u v w x y z

WRITING WORKOUT:

Now it's time to practice writing the Basic Formal Script alphabet on tracing paper, using your flat-tipped calligraphy marker. Paper-clip a sheet of tracing paper over the alphabet below and strive for a consistent pace, using only moderate pressure.

a b c d e f g h i
j k k l m n o p q
r s t u v w x y z

Do your traced letters look like the ones printed above? Keep tracing until you feel comfortable with the alphabet. Then, on the lines on the following page, practice making each letter on your own. (Notice how the ascender and descender lines are closer to the waist and base lines.)

Joining Letters

Read the sentence printed in the Writing Workout on the next page and you'll see that the letters don't join together as they do in the Basic Chancery Italic style. The letters ending in an upward curve almost touch the next letters without actually joining them.

*W*RITING WORKOUT:

Are you ready to make a complete sentence? The first time you trace the sentence on the next page, draw the letter o in between each word so that you get a feel for the amount of space needed. Once you feel comfortable with the spacing, you can practice tracing the sentence without the o placeholders.
Calligraphy will only get easier with practice, so trace this exercise until you feel comfortable with each letter.

success is getting

what you want;

happiness is wanting

what you get.

Now it's your turn! On the lines below, write the sentence you just traced. Take your time, and refer to the above illustration for guidance.

Gift Tags with Class

Give all your presents homemade panache when you top them off with calligraphy gift tags!

MATERIALS:

- pencil
- ruler
- one piece of construction paper cut into strips, 1½ inches wide by 5 inches long for each gift
- black calligraphy marker
- scratch paper
- soft eraser
- hole puncher
- colorful yarn, cut into 4-inch-long pieces

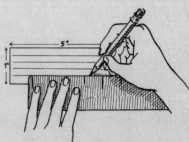

DIRECTIONS:

1. First you need to create guidelines on each gift tag for proper spacing of your lettering. With your pencil and ruler, draw four lines on each tag using the lines below as a guide. (The guidelines are for Basic Formal Script.)

----

2. Now, with your calligraphy marker, practice writing your first name and each person's first name on a sheet of scratch paper. Also, practice writing "To:" and "From:". When your letters look good to you, center your message on the gift tags (To: [your friend's first name] From: [your first name]). Wait at least 30 minutes for the ink to dry and then erase the pencil lines.

3. When you're finished addressing the gift tags, use the hole puncher to put a hole in the left-hand corner of each one. Then thread a piece of colorful yarn through each hole and fasten the tag to the package. You can tie the yarn around the bow or ribbon.

The Numbers Game

The Basic Formal Script does not have its own set of numerals, but Arabic numerals look great paired with this calligraphy style, because both have a somewhat heavy look. Notice that the numerals *1, 2,* and *0* sit directly on the base line and will fill the space between the waist and base lines just like the lowercase letter *o.* The numerals *3, 4, 5, 7,* and *9* fall below the base line, and the numerals *6* and *8* rise above the waist line.

*W*RITING WORKOUT:

Trace the Arabic numerals below with your calligraphy marker.

Once you're familiar with the numbers, on the lines below draw the numerals 0 through 9 on your own.

Fantastic Folded Notecards

This beautiful personalized stationery can be used to send messages to your special buddies.

MATERIALS:
- tracing paper
- black calligraphy marker
- 10 sheets of 8½-by-11-inch stationery paper
- scissors
- pencil
- ruler
- soft eraser

DIRECTIONS:

1. First you need to practice writing your name in calligraphy using the Basic Formal Script hand. Trace the guidelines in step 4 on the next page onto tracing paper. Using your calligraphy marker, then trace your name using the alphabet on page 32. Keep tracing and practicing until you've got the hang of writing your name.

2. Now you need to trace, then practice writing, "from the brilliant mind of [your name]." You'll put this phrase at the top of each notecard.

from the brilliant

mind of

3. Fold each sheet of paper in half widthwise to create a wide rectangle. Be sure to fold the crease hard. Open up each piece of paper and carefully cut along the center line. When you have finished cutting all 10 sheets, you'll have 20 notecards, each 8½ inches wide by 5½ inches long.

4. With the pencil and ruler, measure out and lightly draw the guidelines across the top center of each piece of paper. Use the lines below as a guide. These guidelines will help you as you write "from the brilliant mind of" and your name in calligraphy. (You may need to make two sets of lines if all the words won't fit on the first set.)

_____

_____
----

5. Take your time writing the copy line on each piece of paper. Be sure to leave a letter o space between each word. When you're done writing, allow the ink to dry, then carefully erase the lined pencil marks. When you're finished, you'll have personalized, homemade notecards on which to write messages, poems, or any kind of greeting (in calligraphy, of course!) to friends and family everywhere!

Take this tip:
Personalize the notecards and give them to a couple of special friends or family members. They will be delighted to see their names printed in calligraphy that you wrote yourself! As always, practice, practice, practice first, then create the real thing.

CHAPTER 4

Advanced Calligraphy Lettering

Now that you know the basics, let's move on to some new material that will further your newfound artistic skills. Here are lots of fun and exciting ways to create calligraphy that will really stand out! In this section, the techniques for the decorative Gothic alphabet (also known as Old English) are described, as well as hollow and illuminated lettering, ornamental line finishings, and the use of color to highlight your designs. In addition, you'll receive some great tips for creating your very own alphabet!

The Gothic Alphabet

Gothic letters have a distinctive look created by even, vertical letter forms. In the past, the Gothic hand was most commonly used for formal book-writing, because calligraphers could fit more words on a page than with other alphabet forms. (Notice how long and narrow each lowercase letter is drawn.)

WRITING WORKOUT:

Study the letters on the next page, noticing the distinct flourishes—that is, decorative touches—on the uppercase alphabet. Paper-clip a sheet of tracing paper over first the lowercase alphabet, then the uppercase letters, and use your calligraphy marker to trace over each letter. Continue practicing until you have familiarized yourself with the Gothic alphabet.

abcdefghijkl

mnopqrstuv

wxyz

ABCDEF

GHIJKLM

NOPQRS

TUVWXYZ

Once you feel comfortable tracing the letters, practice making them yourself on the following page. Pull out a writing assignment from social studies, English, or any favorite school subject and copy a paragraph onto the lines on the next page. Refer to the printed letters above for direction, and have fun creating the Gothic alphabet. You'll be surprised how much fun homework can be when you give it a creative calligraphy touch!

Party Time! Invitations

Surprise your pals with these colorful handmade party invitations that are truly original.

MATERIALS:

- your favorite rubber stamp
- ink pad in a color that complements your colored felt marker
- sheet of white, 8½-by-11-inch paper for each invited guest
- pencil
- ruler
- your black calligraphy marker
- one colored flat-tipped felt marker (red, green, orange, blue, or purple)
- scratch paper
- soft eraser

DIRECTIONS:

1. First create your own custom paper. To do this, press your favorite rubber stamp onto the colored ink pad and carefully apply the stamp all around the edge of the 8½-by-11-inch sheet of paper as shown. Let the ink dry for 30 minutes.

2. Using the sample on the next page, center one practice invitation over the lines and trace them lightly with your pencil and ruler. If the invitation paper is too thick to see through, you will have to use your ruler to measure out the lines onto the invitations. Write all the important party information on the practice invitation to make sure

it will fit on the lines provided. Where needed, add an additional set of lines. Once you are happy with how the party details fit, lightly draw in the guidelines on the other invitations.

Who:

What:

When:

Where:

RSVP:

3. Go back and study the Gothic alphabet on page 40. Trace over the letters again for more practice. Then, on scratch paper, practice writing *Who, What, Where, When,* and *RSVP* with your calligraphy marker. Once you've mastered the letters, use your colored calligraphy marker to write *Who, What, Where, When,* and *RSVP,* each on its own line, on your invitations.

4. Next, on a sheet of scratch paper, practice lettering the details of the invitation (name of the guest of honor; reason for the party; the time, date, and place; and finally the RSVP phone number), which

all need to be filled in on the penciled lines of your custom paper. Use either the Basic Chancery Italic or Basic Formal Script style. When you're comfortable with your lettering, transfer all the information onto each party invitation.

5. Let the ink dry for at least 30 minutes, then carefully erase the pencil lines. Now you've got party invitations that partygoers are sure to love!

Ornamental Letters

Ornamental or decorative lettering and designs will enhance any calligraphy project you do.

ornamental letter

The following exercises focus on illuminated lettering, which are letters decorated with colorful designs or illustrations.

You will begin with basic Roman capital letters. While the height of these letters is the same, the width of each letter will vary. For example, the letter *I* will take up less space than the letter *W*.

*W*RITING WORKOUT:

Study the practice letters on the following page. Notice that the *A, B, H, N, S, T, U, V, X, Y,* and *Z* are ¾ inch wide, but *C, D, G, M, O, Q,* and *W* are 1 inch wide. The other letters, *E, F, I, J, K, L, P,* and *R,* are only ½ inch wide.

On page 46, use a straight-tipped (not flat-tipped) black nylon pen to practice drawing the letters in the boxes on page 45. Pay close attention to the width of each letter and use a ruler to try to make the size and shape the same as in the above illustration. It's important to become comfortable with the different sizes before going on to add decorations.

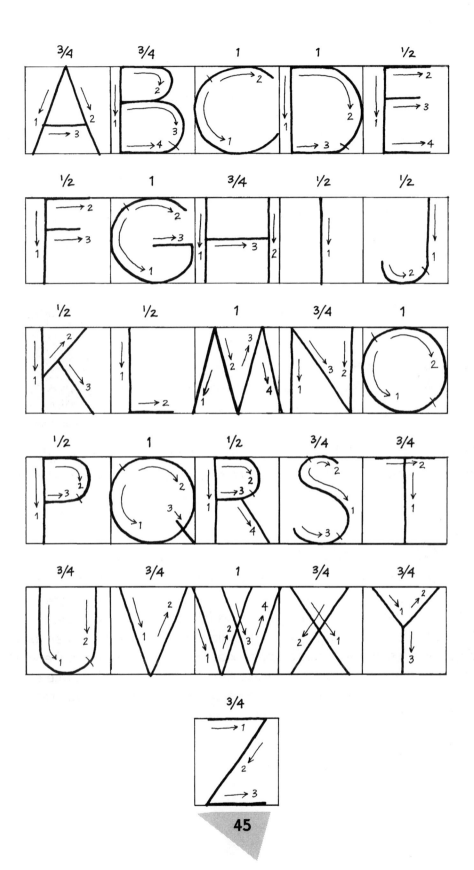

With decorated letters, you will begin with the basic Roman letter format. The letters are then thickened, or built up, in order to make a place to add color. To build up these letters, you will add an extra line or two to the side of each letter. This will leave a white space in the middle of the letter that can be colored in. To know where to put the new line, follow the illustrations on the next page, and with a straight-tipped black nylon pen add additional lines to the Roman alphabet you drew above.

Once you've built up all the letters on page 46, fill the thickened areas with color. You can fill in the space with one solid color, or use stripes, polka dots, or anything else you can imagine!

A B C D E

F G H I J

K L M N

O P Q R

S T U V W

X Y Z

To School with Style

Make homework more exciting with a personalized notebook and pencil holder!

MATERIALS:

- scissors
- two sheets of 8½-by-11-inch construction paper in your favorite color
- empty, clean juice can
- pencil
- 8½-by-11-inch spiral notebook in your favorite color
- tape measure (or ruler)
- scratch paper
- calligraphy brush marker
- glue

DIRECTIONS:

1. First you need to use scissors to trim the construction paper to a smaller rectangle that will fit around the juice can. To do this, measure the height of the juice can just below the top lip down to the bottom. Use a pencil to mark that same measurement on your construction paper. Next, measure the can around the circumference and add ⅛ inch. Make pencil marks on your paper to that same measurement. You should now have a rectangle that will fit around the can. Finally, cut out the rectangular shape and set it aside.

2. Take the second sheet of construction paper and measure in 1½ inches around the entire border. Cut it so that the sheet is 7 inches wide by 9½ inches long. This sheet will be used to cover your spiral notebook. Set this aside as well, as you perfect your monogrammed calligraphy.

3. On scratch paper, practice lettering your initials using the Gothic capital letters. (You may choose to illuminate your letters, which make for great-looking monograms. See page 47 for illuminated letters.) Then, on the lines below, practice centering your letters. Decide now which subject you'll use the notebook for, such as reading or science, and practice lettering the name of the class.

4. Once you feel comfortable with your style, you're ready to write on the paper with your brush pen. Carefully monogram your initials on the center of the sheet to cover your notebook. In the same calligraphy style, write the name of the subject in the top-right corner of the paper. Then monogram your initials on the center of the paper that you cut for the juice can. Allow the ink to dry.

5. Once the sheets are dry, apply glue to the back side of the 7-by-9½-inch sheet of paper. Carefully center the paper on the notebook, and you'll be left with a cool colored border around the edges! Press into place. Next apply glue to the back side of the paper for the juice can. Place the paper on the can and roll it onto the surface, making sure all the edges are firmly glued down. Let the glue dry for several hours before using. Now you're ready to go to class with a little class!

Take this tip:
To add even more pizazz to your designs, you can create eye-catching borders around the edges of the pencil holder and notebook using a different-color ink. See page 14 to learn how to create calligraphy borders.

Ornamental Line Finishes

A line finish is a small, artistic design or squiggle that is placed either at the end of a document or throughout a piece of calligraphy. A decorative line finish will make your artwork look special, or it can give a calligrapher's signature an unusual, one-of-a-kind look. The designs can also be linked together to create a border, to highlight important words or phrases, or to add a finishing touch to a sentence or paragraph.

    Use your calligraphy marker to form all of the following line finishes.

WRITING WORKOUT:

DOTS: Single dots or groups of dots can enhance any part of a document.

    These dots are drawn as a group of four in a diamond pattern, but they can also be drawn in groups of three. Study the illustration below, then trace it. Dot number 1 sets the pattern for the rest of the dots to follow. Center each group of dots along the single line provided.

DOTS AND STROKES: A row of dots and strokes is a nice ending for a calligraphy project.

    The dots are drawn as instructed above. The strokes begin on a single line, then drop slightly below and end up again on that line. First trace the dots and strokes, and then draw them on the line below.

DOUBLE STROKES: Double strokes make nice top and bottom borders.

The top row of strokes is drawn just above a single line; the bottom row is drawn between and just underneath the line. Study the stroke first, then practice drawing freehand on the line below.

THE SPIRAL: The spiral is ideal to use as a border down the left or right side of your document.

To create a spiral, draw an upper and a lower guideline with a ¼-inch space in between. The spiral stroke begins slightly below the upper guideline. It swoops up to touch the line, then crosses back down to barely touch the bottom guideline. First study the strokes, then practice drawing them freehand. For best results, try to form each line of the spiral in one fluid motion.

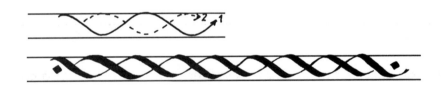

Give It Color

Add interest to your hand-lettered messages with a colored flat-tipped marker. If you decide to use color, follow the suggestions below.

- For the most elegant appearance, use no more than two colors in one document (usually black and one other color). The use of too many colors will take attention away from the meaning of the text and diminish the natural beauty of the calligraphy.

- Red is the brightest and most striking color. You can use red whenever you want to catch someone's eye.

- Avoid clashing color combinations. Usually a dark and a light color will look nice together.

- A surefire way to grab the reader's attention is to use colored ink on only the first uppercase letter of the message. (This is also a good place to create a colorful illuminated letter.) For example, in a piece of artwork beginning with "Once upon a time," you'd use colored ink for the uppercase *O*.

Design It Yourself!

When it comes to calligraphy, you don't always have to follow the rules. Below are some helpful suggestions and basic steps for creating your individual style of calligraphy. Put your imagination into high gear and have fun creating your own personalized alphabet!

MATERIALS:
- black calligraphy marker
- tracing paper or scratch paper
- pencil
- ruler

DIRECTIONS:

1. Go over the Basic Chancery Italic alphabet on page 17 and compare it with the Basic Formal Script style on page 32. Do you notice how the Chancery hand slants to the right and the Script style is straight up and down? Even that small change completely alters the look of the two alphabets. Study how the slant or size changes the artwork. With your pen, make a very round letter *o*; then a tall, narrow *o*; and finally a short, oval *o*.

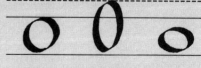

_____

_____

_____

_____

2. Now, using the first round *o* as a guide, practice drawing all 26 lowercase letters of the alphabet on the lines above, making each letter as round as you can.

3. Using the second tall, narrow *o* as a guide, practice making each letter of the alphabet tall and narrow.

4. Using the oval *o* as an example, draw the alphabet again, making each letter oval-shaped.

5. Look at the three styles you've created. See how different they look? Now you've got a foundation for creating your very own style! Choose your favorite style from the three choices above and adapt it to suit your personal taste by adding small or large hooks or flourishes. If you need more space for writing, with your pencil and ruler lightly trace the guidelines below on a sheet of tracing paper. Continue finessing your alphabet until you are pleased with every letter. Once you've come up with a new, unique alphabet, teach your calligraphy-loving friends how to do it.

_____

_____

_____

_____

_____

_____

CHAPTER 5

Putting It All Together

N ow that you've learned several calligraphy alphabets as well as some decorative techniques, you're ready to focus on some simple rules on layout and design. This chapter also includes tips on spacing, centering, and keeping your lines straight.

Using Design in Calligraphy

A design deals with the "look" of a project. It can make a piece of art look hip and cool, classic and old-fashioned, or weird and wacky. When you create a design, the arrangement and size of words and letters, the colors used, and even the type of paper all factor into the overall appearance of the finished product. And yet there is only one deciding factor for design in calligraphy: what looks good to the calligrapher's eye.

For example, the following quote can be laid out to fit a number of designs.

"The most I can do for my friend is to be his friend."

—Thoreau

"The most
I can do for
my friend
is to be
his friend."

THOREAU

"The most
I can do
for my friend
is to be
his friend."
Thoreau

"The most I can
do for my friend
is to be his friend."

❖ Thoreau ❖

Notice how each design changes the way the quote looks on paper. So how can you learn to achieve the effect you want for your own work?

Think about words you see every day in newspapers and magazines, on television, on T-shirts, in advertisements, and on things you buy in a store. Where possible, cut out pictures of word designs that appeal to you and keep them in a folder that you can look at for ideas when you are planning your next masterpiece. Don't feel you have to copy something exactly as you've seen it done before. The real fun in doing calligraphy projects is creating something original and especially your own.

Spacing Between Letters and Words

While there is no clear-cut rule on the amount of spacing necessary, each word should look evenly spaced, and all of the words in a single document should have even spacing between unjoined letters.

Spacing between words will be dictated by the type of document and the amount of lettering on a page. In general, you should allow a $\frac{1}{2}$-inch space between each word and an $\frac{1}{8}$-inch space between each letter. Try to achieve a balance so that there is neither a lot of white space nor a crowded feeling between words. Let your eye be the judge.

Getting It Straight

The trick to making your lettering straight on unlined paper without penciling in lines is to place guide sheets under the paper on which you are working. This will allow the lines to show through while you are lettering but not show through when you are done.

To make your own guide sheet you will need: two sheets of good quality, unlined $8\frac{1}{2}$-by-11-inch paper; two sheets of lined, wide-ruled notebook paper; a pencil with a soft eraser; a fine-point black nylon-tipped pen; a ruler; and paper clips or drafting tape.

To make guide-sheet one: Guide-sheet one will have lines a $\frac{1}{2}$ inch apart and can be used for projects with lettering of this size. On one unlined sheet of paper, use the pencil and the ruler to draw horizontal lines (from side to side) a $\frac{1}{2}$ inch apart across the page, all the way down. Once you have marked the lines in pencil, use the ruler and black nylon-tipped pen to darken and trace over these lines. Allow the black lines to dry.

To make guide-sheet two: Guide-sheet two will have wider lines. Use this guide sheet when you want to make larger letters. With the black nylon-tipped pen and ruler, draw along the top line on one lined sheet of notebook paper. Skip the second line, then draw along the third line. Continue drawing along the lines, skipping every other line. This will give you a guide sheet with lines approximately $1\frac{1}{16}$ inches apart.

To use either guide sheet, position it underneath the paper on which you plan to letter. Use a few paper clips or drafting tape to stick the two pages together so they don't drift apart while you are working. The lines from your guide sheet will show through the paper you are lettering on and will help to keep your words in a straight line.

Guide sheets do not work when the calligraphy paper is too thick to see through. In this case, you will have to use a ruler and a pencil to lightly draw in the guidelines. Then, once the ink has dried, erase all pencil lines.

Centering Made Simple

To make a guide sheet for centering words, such as titles, on paper, start with an 8 ½-by-11-inch unlined sheet of paper. Fold the paper in half lengthwise and in half again widthwise to create creases. Unfold the paper.

With a black nylon-tipped pen and a ruler, draw a vertical line (from top to bottom) down the long crease on the page. Next draw a horizontal line across, on the second crease on the page.

Once the ink has dried, place this centering page beneath a practice piece of paper. You will then use the practice sheet as your guide for the actual piece.

To center a whole document: Count the number of lines you have planned for your document. Pencil in the middle line first. For example, if you have five lines to draw, line number three would be in the exact middle of your document. If you have an even number of lines, for instance eight, the middle would be between lines four and five. The higher number—in this case, line five—should be centered. Pencil the words of this line on the dark middle line. Next, with a ruler, divide the space above and below this middle line and pencil in the words for each of those lines. It doesn't matter how much space you allow for each line, as long as the writing doesn't look cramped. Remember, this is just a rough draft. If you make a mistake, you can simply erase it and try again.

To center the words on each line: Count the number of letters and spaces for each line. The center letter of the line will go on the vertical center line of the guide sheet. For instance, if you want to center the phrase *Happy Birthday!* first count the letters and spaces. There are fifteen characters including the word space and the exclamation point, and the center one is the letter *i.* Put *i* on the vertical center line, then continue adding the rest of the letters on either side. If the center of a line is in between two letters, put the two letters on either side of the vertical guideline. Be sure to allow extra room for the wider letters, such as *C, D, G, M, O, Q,* and *W.* The thinner letters, *I, T, J, F,* and *L,* will take up less space. Use your eye to judge exactly how much space to leave for each letter.

Once you have finished the rough pencil draft, take a few moments to look it over. Does the design look crowded, too spread out, or just right? Keep working on your words and letters until they look good to you. Finally, place the practice sheet under your calligraphy paper and use it as a guide to ink in your letters.

The Birthday Poster Surprise
Make a friend's or family member's birthday a big deal with this awesome birthday proclamation!

MATERIALS:

- paper clips
- tracing paper
- pencil
- guide sheet for centering (directions on page 58)
- unlined stationery paper (thin enough to see through)
- black calligraphy marker
- colored poster board
- soft eraser
- black nylon-tipped pen
- ruler
- scissors
- glue

T o: _____

_____

was a very good day
in history
'cuz you were born.

Happy Birthday!

The birthday proclamation will read as follows:

To: [name]
[month, day, year]
was a very good day
in history
'cuz you were born.
Happy Birthday!

DIRECTIONS:

1. Paper-clip the tracing paper over the birthday proclamation shown above and, with the pencil, trace the words. Don't forget to leave a space for the name and birth date of your friend. The purpose of making a practice sketch in pencil is to help you judge where to begin and end each line and how wide the letters should be.

2. Pull out the guide sheet for centering and paper-clip it underneath the tracing paper. In pencil, sketch in the name and birth date of your friend on the tracing paper, using the directions for centering words on a line on page 58. Remember that wide letters like *M* and *W* will require twice the space of other letters, and that the letter *I* and the number *1*, which are thin, will require less space.

3. Once you have completed the practice sketch in pencil, you can move on to create your finished product. Place the practice sketch underneath your stationery paper. Using the penciled letters underneath as a guide, pick your favorite style of calligraphy to draw over the letters with your black calligraphy marker. You may even want to use illuminated lettering for the first letter in each row or for the birthday person's name. If you do, use the black nylon-tipped pen for outlining, the colored pencils to fill in. You may also want to add a lively border design along the top and bottom of the proclamation.

4. Set aside the calligraphy piece to dry. Meanwhile, with a ruler, measure a piece of colored poster board 4 inches wider and 4 inches taller than the proclamation. Cut it out.

5. When the calligraphy is dry, carefully glue it onto the poster board. You should have a colorful 2-inch border all the way around your birthday sign. Brighten up your poster by adding color to the border designs or any illuminated letters.

Displaying Your Calligraphy

Once you have completed a calligraphy piece, such as the birthday proclamation on page 60, you'll want to display it proudly.

Because calligraphy is ornate, a simple wood or metal frame works best. For a small piece of calligraphy (under 4 inches), you can choose a larger frame with a mat, which is an inside border usually made of stiff cardboard. Generally, a 2-inch mat that allows an even amount of white space around the document is recommended. A larger, full-page calligraphy piece will look fine in a plain frame without a mat.

Framed calligraphy looks best when there is a natural border of white space—at least $\frac{3}{4}$ inch—on all sides between the frame and where the lettering starts. If you are planning to frame a piece, it is a good idea to plan the size of the finished piece during the designing process so that you allow enough room for the frame *plus* at least a $\frac{3}{4}$-inch border of white paper.

On Your Own

Now that you have learned the basics of calligraphy, you are ready to strike out on your own and find ways to use your newfound talent. Here are a few suggestions to get you started.

- Use calligraphy to personalize your homework assignments. Jazz up your school presentations with the illuminated lettering techniques and fun border designs.

- With large sheets of butcher paper, you can make your own beautiful wrapping paper. Use your brush pen to write an appropriate phrase such as

"Happy Birthday!" several times all over the paper. Tie up the package with several colorful ribbons.

- Create an interesting design for your monogram and write it on your book bag or backpack.

- Use calligraphy to label your tapes and CDs, giving your music collection an organized but artistic air.

What else can you do? The sky's the limit, so get creative and keep on writing!

HAVE FUN with CALLIGRAPHY!